The Biggest Kink List For Your Sex Life!

Read all the rules and definitions of Kinks and fill in the blanks according to your interest.

Also get a copy for your partner, and have them do the same. Finally, you can show each other your lists and talk about them or participate in these activities.

We suggest that you try new Kinks together, or let your partner choose your Kink without telling you, and do the same in the next session.

Have an unforgettable time!

Bucket List for Your Sex Life!

There is a special tick next to every kink, fetish and activity like this: Humiliation ✓

You can only tick activities that you did for your partner, or that you both did: Humiliation ✔

If there is an activity that is only for one person, for example: Blowjob ✓   then your partner ticks it because he did it, and you also tick it because you participated in it, and you can't do it for your partner. Blowjob ✔

My Biggest Kink List

Name: _____   Date: _____

RULES

Fill every bar of Kink,
based on Your interests

How to fill it?

That's my Limit	⊗
Let's Try	✦
If You want	☆
I like it	☆ ☆
I Love it!	☆ ☆ ☆
FUCK YESSS!	☆ ☆ ☆ ♥
DONE ON MY BUCKET LIST	✓

Assume that you are a
submissive part of every kink

example:
⊗ You reject to recive it
⊗☆☆☆♥ You crave to recive it!

FUNDAMENTALS

Should we mention this?

Cuddling ⊗ ☆☆☆☆ ♡

Kissing ⊗ ☆☆☆☆ ♡

Petting ✓⊗ ☆☆☆☆ ♡

Handjob ✓⊗ ☆☆☆☆ ♡

Cunnilingus ✓⊗ ☆☆☆☆ ♡

Blowjob ✓⊗ ☆☆☆☆ ♡

Vanilla Sex ✓⊗ ☆☆☆☆ ♡

Wanna Kiss?

Neck Kisses ✓⊗ ☆☆☆☆ ♡

Body Kisses ✓⊗ ☆☆☆☆ ♡

Feet Kisses ✓⊗ ☆☆☆☆ ♡

Breast/Chest Kisses ✓⊗ ☆☆☆☆ ♡

Belly Kisses ✓⊗ ☆☆☆☆ ♡

French Kisses ✓⊗ ☆☆☆☆ ♡

Upside Down Kisses ✓⊗ ☆☆☆☆ ♡

_____ ✓⊗ ☆☆☆☆ ♡

FUNDAMENTALS

Bite me like a Vampire!

Biting ✓ⓧ✖☆☆☆☆♡

Neck Biting ✓ⓧ✖☆☆☆☆♡

Body Biting ✓ⓧ✖☆☆☆☆♡

Lips Biting ✓ⓧ✖☆☆☆☆♡

Nipples Biting ✓ⓧ✖☆☆☆☆♡

Penis Biting ✓ⓧ✖☆☆☆☆♡

_____ ✓ⓧ✖☆☆☆☆♡

I hope You played a lot on Console...

Fingering ✓ⓧ✖☆☆☆☆♡

One Finger Petting ✓ⓧ✖☆☆☆☆♡

One Finger Teasing ✓ⓧ✖☆☆☆☆♡

Fingers Sucking ✓ⓧ✖☆☆☆☆♡

Finger in Butt ✓ⓧ✖☆☆☆☆♡

Touching with Glove ✓ⓧ✖☆☆☆☆♡

_____ ✓ⓧ✖☆☆☆☆♡

YOU ARE SO NAUGHTY...

Deepthroat ✓⊗ ✶☆☆☆☆♡

Swallowing ✓⊗ ✶☆☆☆☆♡

Facial ✓⊗ ✶☆☆☆☆♡

Balls licking ✓⊗ ✶☆☆☆☆♡

Facesitting ✓⊗ ✶☆☆☆☆♡

Edging ✓⊗ ✶☆☆☆☆♡

Rough Sex ✓⊗ ✶☆☆☆☆♡

Anal Sex ✓⊗ ✶☆☆☆☆♡

Dirty Talk ✓⊗ ✶☆☆☆☆♡

Spanking ✓⊗ ✶☆☆☆☆♡

Gagging ✓⊗ ✶☆☆☆☆♡

Orgasm Control ✓⊗ ✶☆☆☆☆♡

Ruined Orgasm ✓⊗ ✶☆☆☆☆♡

Tease and Denial ✓⊗ ✶☆☆☆☆♡

Humiliation ✓⊗ ✶☆☆☆☆♡

Praise kink ✓⊗ ✶☆☆☆☆♡

Degradation kink ✓⊗ ✶☆☆☆☆♡

_____ ✓⊗ ✶☆☆☆☆♡

_____ ✓⊗ ✶☆☆☆☆♡

ONLY FOR BRAVE ONES

Tied Up ✓ ⊗ ✫ ☆ ☆ ☆ ♡

Rim Job ✓ ⊗ ✫ ☆ ☆ ☆ ♡

Hot Wax play ✓ ⊗ ✫ ☆ ☆ ☆ ♡

Heat Play ✓ ⊗ ✫ ☆ ☆ ☆ ♡

Cold Play ✓ ⊗ ✫ ☆ ☆ ☆ ♡

Golden Shower ✓ ⊗ ✫ ☆ ☆ ☆ ♡

Discomfort during sex ✓ ⊗ ✫ ☆ ☆ ☆ ♡

Sweat ✓ ⊗ ✫ ☆ ☆ ☆ ♡

Multiple Orgasms ✓ ⊗ ✫ ☆ ☆ ☆ ♡

Watching Porn ✓ ⊗ ✫ ☆ ☆ ☆ ♡

Rim Job ✓ ⊗ ✫ ☆ ☆ ☆ ♡

_____ ✓ ⊗ ✫ ☆ ☆ ☆ ♡

_____ ✓ ⊗ ✫ ☆ ☆ ☆ ♡

_____ ✓ ⊗ ✫ ☆ ☆ ☆ ♡

FUCK ME HARD

Face Slapping ✓ ⊗ ✶ ☆ ☆ ☆ ♡

Choking ✓ ⊗ ✶ ☆ ☆ ☆ ♡

Fighting Sex ✓ ⊗ ✶ ☆ ☆ ☆ ♡

Scratching ✓ ⊗ ✶ ☆ ☆ ☆ ♡

Loud Sex ✓ ⊗ ✶ ☆ ☆ ☆ ♡

Hate Sex ✓ ⊗ ✶ ☆ ☆ ☆ ♡

Power Play ✓ ⊗ ✶ ☆ ☆ ☆ ♡

Breath Play ✓ ⊗ ✶ ☆ ☆ ☆ ♡

CBT ✓ ⊗ ✶ ☆ ☆ ☆ ♡

Punishments ✓ ⊗ ✶ ☆ ☆ ☆ ♡

Face-fucking ✓ ⊗ ✶ ☆ ☆ ☆ ♡

Fisting ✓ ⊗ ✶ ☆ ☆ ☆ ♡

Pegging ✓ ⊗ ✶ ☆ ☆ ☆ ♡

Boobs Torture ✓ ⊗ ✶ ☆ ☆ ☆ ♡

Forced Sex ✓ ⊗ ✶ ☆ ☆ ☆ ♡

_____ ✓ ⊗ ✶ ☆ ☆ ☆ ♡

_____ ✓ ⊗ ✶ ☆ ☆ ☆ ♡

_____ ✓ ⊗ ✶ ☆ ☆ ☆ ♡

YOU ARE UNIQUE

Sensation Play ✓ ⊗ ✗ ☆ ☆ ☆ ☆ ♡

WAM Play ✓ ⊗ ✗ ☆ ☆ ☆ ☆ ♡

Body painting ✓ ⊗ ✗ ☆ ☆ ☆ ☆ ♡

Shibari ✓ ⊗ ✗ ☆ ☆ ☆ ☆ ♡

Nyotaimori ✓ ⊗ ✗ ☆ ☆ ☆ ☆ ♡

Ahegao ✓ ⊗ ✗ ☆ ☆ ☆ ☆ ♡

Food Play ✓ ⊗ ✗ ☆ ☆ ☆ ☆ ♡

Cyber Sex ✓ ⊗ ✗ ☆ ☆ ☆ ☆ ♡

Cage Play ✓ ⊗ ✗ ☆ ☆ ☆ ☆ ♡

JOI ✓ ⊗ ✗ ☆ ☆ ☆ ☆ ♡

Body Worship ✓ ⊗ ✗ ☆ ☆ ☆ ☆ ♡

Coming without
being touched ✓ ⊗ ✗ ☆ ☆ ☆ ☆ ♡

Erotic Furniture ✓ ⊗ ✗ ☆ ☆ ☆ ☆ ♡

_____ ✓ ⊗ ✗ ☆ ☆ ☆ ☆ ♡

_____ ✓ ⊗ ✗ ☆ ☆ ☆ ☆ ♡

_____ ✓ ⊗ ✗ ☆ ☆ ☆ ☆ ♡

MY PREFERENCES

a Top ✓ ⊗ ✦ ☆ ☆ ☆ ☆ ♡

a Bottom ✓ ⊗ ✦ ☆ ☆ ☆ ☆ ♡

DDLG ✓ ⊗ ✦ ☆ ☆ ☆ ☆ ♡

MDLB ✓ ⊗ ✦ ☆ ☆ ☆ ☆ ♡

24/7 ✓ ⊗ ✦ ☆ ☆ ☆ ☆ ♡

Dominant ✓ ⊗ ✦ ☆ ☆ ☆ ☆ ♡

Submissive ✓ ⊗ ✦ ☆ ☆ ☆ ☆ ♡

Pet Play ✓ ⊗ ✦ ☆ ☆ ☆ ☆ ♡

Slave ✓ ⊗ ✦ ☆ ☆ ☆ ☆ ♡

Sugar Mommy/Daddy ✓ ⊗ ✦ ☆ ☆ ☆ ☆ ♡

Switch ✓ ⊗ ✦ ☆ ☆ ☆ ☆ ♡

_____ ✓ ⊗ ✦ ☆ ☆ ☆ ☆ ♡

_____ ✓ ⊗ ✦ ☆ ☆ ☆ ☆ ♡

_____ ✓ ⊗ ✦ ☆ ☆ ☆ ☆ ♡

LET'S ACT LIKE...

Porn Star ✓ ⊗ ★ ☆ ☆ ☆ ♡

School Girl/Boy ✓ ⊗ ★ ☆ ☆ ☆ ♡

Teacher and Student ✓ ⊗ ★ ☆ ☆ ☆ ♡

Erotic Massage Therapist ✓ ⊗ ★ ☆ ☆ ☆ ♡

Police and Burglar ✓ ⊗ ★ ☆ ☆ ☆ ♡

Private Maid/Cleaner ✓ ⊗ ★ ☆ ☆ ☆ ♡

Boss and Employee ✓ ⊗ ★ ☆ ☆ ☆ ♡

Famous singer and the Fan ✓ ⊗ ★ ☆ ☆ ☆ ♡

Doctor and Nurse ✓ ⊗ ★ ☆ ☆ ☆ ♡

Stars of the Movie ✓ ⊗ ★ ☆ ☆ ☆ ♡

Strangers ✓ ⊗ ★ ☆ ☆ ☆ ♡

Femdom/Maledom ✓ ⊗ ★ ☆ ☆ ☆ ♡

Stripper and Customer ✓ ⊗ ★ ☆ ☆ ☆ ♡

_____ ✓ ⊗ ★ ☆ ☆ ☆ ♡

_____ ✓ ⊗ ★ ☆ ☆ ☆ ♡

_____ ✓ ⊗ ★ ☆ ☆ ☆ ♡

_____ ✓ ⊗ ★ ☆ ☆ ☆ ♡

_____ ✓ ⊗ ★ ☆ ☆ ☆ ♡

CALL ME YOUR...

Daddy ✓ ⊗ ✪ ☆ ☆ ☆ ♡

Mommy ✓ ⊗ ✪ ☆ ☆ ☆ ♡

Mistress ✓ ⊗ ✪ ☆ ☆ ☆ ♡

Master ✓ ⊗ ✪ ☆ ☆ ☆ ♡

Princess ✓ ⊗ ✪ ☆ ☆ ☆ ♡

Bitch ✓ ⊗ ✪ ☆ ☆ ☆ ♡

Whore ✓ ⊗ ✪ ☆ ☆ ☆ ♡

Slut ✓ ⊗ ✪ ☆ ☆ ☆ ♡

Fuck Toy ✓ ⊗ ✪ ☆ ☆ ☆ ♡

_____ ✓ ⊗ ✪ ☆ ☆ ☆ ♡

_____ ✓ ⊗ ✪ ☆ ☆ ☆ ♡

_____ ✓ ⊗ ✪ ☆ ☆ ☆ ♡

MY SAFE WORDS

Stop ✓ ⊗ ✪ ☆ ☆ ☆ ♡

Red ✓ ⊗ ✪ ☆ ☆ ☆ ♡

_____ ✓ ⊗ ✪ ☆ ☆ ☆ ♡

_____ ✓ ⊗ ✪ ☆ ☆ ☆ ♡

WHERE YOU WANT TO...?

		✓	⊗	✗	☆	☆	☆	☆	♡
at Home		✓	⊗	✗	☆	☆	☆	☆	♡
Car		✓	⊗	✗	☆	☆	☆	☆	♡
In the Water		✓	⊗	✗	☆	☆	☆	☆	♡
Fitting Room		✓	⊗	✗	☆	☆	☆	☆	♡
Public		✓	⊗	✗	☆	☆	☆	☆	♡
Nature		✓	⊗	✗	☆	☆	☆	☆	♡
Elevator		✓	⊗	✗	☆	☆	☆	☆	♡
Hotel		✓	⊗	✗	☆	☆	☆	☆	♡
Toilet		✓	⊗	✗	☆	☆	☆	☆	♡
Kitchen		✓	⊗	✗	☆	☆	☆	☆	♡
Shower		✓	⊗	✗	☆	☆	☆	☆	♡
Washing Machine		✓	⊗	✗	☆	☆	☆	☆	♡
Roof		✓	⊗	✗	☆	☆	☆	☆	♡
Balcony		✓	⊗	✗	☆	☆	☆	☆	♡
Abandoned buildings		✓	⊗	✗	☆	☆	☆	☆	♡
_____		✓	⊗	✗	☆	☆	☆	☆	♡
_____		✓	⊗	✗	☆	☆	☆	☆	♡
_____		✓	⊗	✗	☆	☆	☆	☆	♡

LET'S WEAR

Sex in Clothes ✓ ⊗ ★ ☆ ☆ ☆ ♡

Erotic Clothes ✓ ⊗ ★ ☆ ☆ ☆ ♡

School Uniform ✓ ⊗ ★ ☆ ☆ ☆ ♡

Erotic Lingerie ✓ ⊗ ★ ☆ ☆ ☆ ♡

Face Mask ✓ ⊗ ★ ☆ ☆ ☆ ♡

High Heels ✓ ⊗ ★ ☆ ☆ ☆ ♡

Police Costume ✓ ⊗ ★ ☆ ☆ ☆ ♡

Nurse Costume ✓ ⊗ ★ ☆ ☆ ☆ ♡

Latex ✓ ⊗ ★ ☆ ☆ ☆ ♡

Cosplay ✓ ⊗ ★ ☆ ☆ ☆ ♡

Knee socks ✓ ⊗ ★ ☆ ☆ ☆ ♡

Pantyhose ✓ ⊗ ★ ☆ ☆ ☆ ♡

Pyjama ✓ ⊗ ★ ☆ ☆ ☆ ♡

Partner's Clothes ✓ ⊗ ★ ☆ ☆ ☆ ♡

Skirt ✓ ⊗ ★ ☆ ☆ ☆ ♡

_____ ✓ ⊗ ★ ☆ ☆ ☆ ♡

_____ ✓ ⊗ ★ ☆ ☆ ☆ ♡

_____ ✓ ⊗ ★ ☆ ☆ ☆ ♡

SEX TOYS

Vibrators

Wand Vibrator ✓ ⊗ ✶ ☆ ☆ ☆ ♡

Rabbit Vibrator ✓ ⊗ ✶ ☆ ☆ ☆ ♡

G-spot Vibrator ✓ ⊗ ✶ ☆ ☆ ☆ ♡

Clit Vibrator ✓ ⊗ ✶ ☆ ☆ ☆ ♡

Tongue Vibrator ✓ ⊗ ✶ ☆ ☆ ☆ ♡

Finger Vibrator ✓ ⊗ ✶ ☆ ☆ ☆ ♡

Bullet/Egg Vibrator ✓ ⊗ ✶ ☆ ☆ ☆ ♡

Panty Vibrator ✓ ⊗ ✶ ☆ ☆ ☆ ♡

Nipples Vibrator ✓ ⊗ ✶ ☆ ☆ ☆ ♡

Triple Stimulators ✓ ⊗ ✶ ☆ ☆ ☆ ♡

_____ ✓ ⊗ ✶ ☆ ☆ ☆ ♡

_____ ✓ ⊗ ✶ ☆ ☆ ☆ ♡

_____ ✓ ⊗ ✶ ☆ ☆ ☆ ♡

_____ ✓ ⊗ ✶ ☆ ☆ ☆ ♡

_____ ✓ ⊗ ✶ ☆ ☆ ☆ ♡

SEX TOYS

Remote Control Toys

Remote Wand Vibrator ✓ ⊗ ✗ ☆ ☆ ☆ ☆ ♡

Remote Rabbit Vibrator ✓ ⊗ ✗ ☆ ☆ ☆ ☆ ♡

Remote Clit Vibrator ✓ ⊗ ✗ ☆ ☆ ☆ ☆ ♡

Remote Anal Vibrator ✓ ⊗ ✗ ☆ ☆ ☆ ☆ ♡

Remote Male Masturbator ✓ ⊗ ✗ ☆ ☆ ☆ ☆ ♡

_____ ✓ ⊗ ✗ ☆ ☆ ☆ ☆ ♡

_____ ✓ ⊗ ✗ ☆ ☆ ☆ ☆ ♡

_____ ✓ ⊗ ✗ ☆ ☆ ☆ ☆ ♡

Man's Toys

Cock Ring ✓ ⊗ ✗ ☆ ☆ ☆ ☆ ♡

Prostate Massager ✓ ⊗ ✗ ☆ ☆ ☆ ☆ ♡

Sex Doll ✓ ⊗ ✗ ☆ ☆ ☆ ☆ ♡

Pocket Pussy ✓ ⊗ ✗ ☆ ☆ ☆ ☆ ♡

Vibrating Masturbator ✓ ⊗ ✗ ☆ ☆ ☆ ☆ ♡

Penis Pump ✓ ⊗ ✗ ☆ ☆ ☆ ☆ ♡

_____ ✓ ⊗ ✗ ☆ ☆ ☆ ☆ ♡

_____ ✓ ⊗ ✗ ☆ ☆ ☆ ☆ ♡

SEX TOYS

BDSM Toys

Collar ✓⊗ ✶☆☆☆☆ ♡

Blindfold ✓⊗ ✶☆☆☆☆ ♡

Belt ✓⊗ ✶☆☆☆☆ ♡

Handcuffs ✓⊗ ✶☆☆☆☆ ♡

Ropes ✓⊗ ✶☆☆☆☆ ♡

Tape ✓⊗ ✶☆☆☆☆ ♡

Zip Tie ✓⊗ ✶☆☆☆☆ ♡

Whip ✓⊗ ✶☆☆☆☆ ♡

Chastity ✓⊗ ✶☆☆☆☆ ♡

Ball Gag ✓⊗ ✶☆☆☆☆ ♡

Open-mouth Gag ✓⊗ ✶☆☆☆☆ ♡

Electro Play Toys ✓⊗ ✶☆☆☆☆ ♡

Ass Hook ✓⊗ ✶☆☆☆☆ ♡

_____ ✓⊗ ✶☆☆☆☆ ♡

_____ ✓⊗ ✶☆☆☆☆ ♡

_____ ✓⊗ ✶☆☆☆☆ ♡

_____ ✓⊗ ✶☆☆☆☆ ♡

SEX POSITIONS
Man on Top

SEX POSITIONS
Girl on Top

SEX POSITIONS
Standing Position

SEX POSITIONS
Laying Position

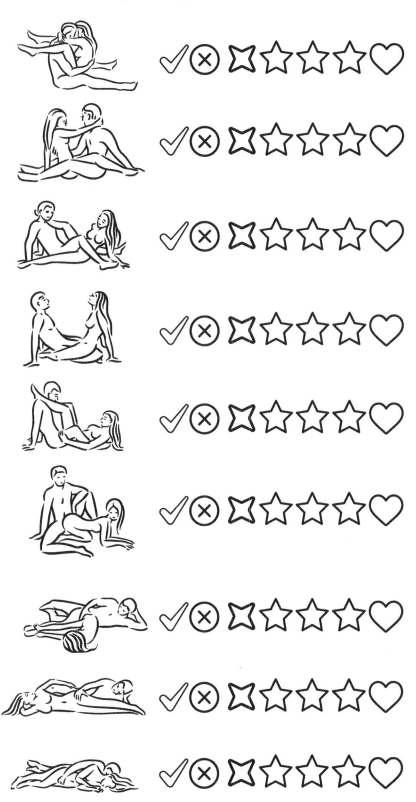

SEX POSITIONS
Oral Sex Position

 ✓ ⊗ ✖ ☆ ☆ ☆ ☆ ♡

 ✓ ⊗ ✖ ☆ ☆ ☆ ☆ ♡

 ✓ ⊗ ✖ ☆ ☆ ☆ ☆ ♡

 ✓ ⊗ ✖ ☆ ☆ ☆ ☆ ♡

 ✓ ⊗ ✖ ☆ ☆ ☆ ☆ ♡

YOUR IDEAS

_____ ✓ ⊗ ✗ ☆ ☆ ☆ ☆ ♡

_____ ✓ ⊗ ✗ ☆ ☆ ☆ ☆ ♡

_____ ✓ ⊗ ✗ ☆ ☆ ☆ ☆ ♡

_____ ✓ ⊗ ✗ ☆ ☆ ☆ ☆ ♡

_____ ✓ ⊗ ✗ ☆ ☆ ☆ ☆ ♡

_____ ✓ ⊗ ✗ ☆ ☆ ☆ ☆ ♡

_____ ✓ ⊗ ✗ ☆ ☆ ☆ ☆ ♡

_____ ✓ ⊗ ✗ ☆ ☆ ☆ ☆ ♡

_____ ✓ ⊗ ✗ ☆ ☆ ☆ ☆ ♡

_____ ✓ ⊗ ✗ ☆ ☆ ☆ ☆ ♡

_____ ✓ ⊗ ✗ ☆ ☆ ☆ ☆ ♡

_____ ✓ ⊗ ✗ ☆ ☆ ☆ ☆ ♡

_____ ✓ ⊗ ✗ ☆ ☆ ☆ ☆ ♡

_____ ✓ ⊗ ✗ ☆ ☆ ☆ ☆ ♡

_____ ✓ ⊗ ✗ ☆ ☆ ☆ ☆ ♡

_____ ✓ ⊗ ✗ ☆ ☆ ☆ ☆ ♡

_____ ✓ ⊗ ✗ ☆ ☆ ☆ ☆ ♡

_____ ✓ ⊗ ✗ ☆ ☆ ☆ ☆ ♡

YOUR IDEAS

_____ ✓ ⊗ ✗ ☆ ☆ ☆ ♡

_____ ✓ ⊗ ✗ ☆ ☆ ☆ ♡

_____ ✓ ⊗ ✗ ☆ ☆ ☆ ♡

_____ ✓ ⊗ ✗ ☆ ☆ ☆ ♡

_____ ✓ ⊗ ✗ ☆ ☆ ☆ ♡

_____ ✓ ⊗ ✗ ☆ ☆ ☆ ♡

_____ ✓ ⊗ ✗ ☆ ☆ ☆ ♡

_____ ✓ ⊗ ✗ ☆ ☆ ☆ ♡

_____ ✓ ⊗ ✗ ☆ ☆ ☆ ♡

_____ ✓ ⊗ ✗ ☆ ☆ ☆ ♡

_____ ✓ ⊗ ✗ ☆ ☆ ☆ ♡

_____ ✓ ⊗ ✗ ☆ ☆ ☆ ♡

_____ ✓ ⊗ ✗ ☆ ☆ ☆ ♡

_____ ✓ ⊗ ✗ ☆ ☆ ☆ ♡

_____ ✓ ⊗ ✗ ☆ ☆ ☆ ♡

_____ ✓ ⊗ ✗ ☆ ☆ ☆ ♡

_____ ✓ ⊗ ✗ ☆ ☆ ☆ ♡

Definitions of Kinks and Fetishes

I HOPE YOU PLAYED A LOT ON CONSOLE...

Fingering - Fingering means that the male partner uses his finger(s) or hand to stimulate the vagina of the female partner

One Finger Petting - sexual activity between partners that does not involve sexual intercourse, such as touching a partner's penis or pussy with a finger while kissing

One Finger Teasing - Playfully arouse sexual passion in your partner by placing your finger on penis or pussy and then denying satisfaction (ejaculation or orgasm)

YOU ARE SO NAUGHTY...

Deepthroat - Deep-throating is when the partner puts as much of his penis into the womans mouth as he can during a blow job, sometimes even the whole penis

Swallowing - When a woman gives her partner a blowjob and then swallows the sperm down her throat.

Facial - when a man ejaculates on the face of his partner.

Balls licking - also known as tea-bagging is the act of taking your partner's testicles into your mouth, often repeated by moving them up and down like a person dips a tea bag

Facesitting - also known as queening, is a sexual practice in which a woman sits on or over her partner's face, typically to facilitate or force oral-genital or oral-anal contact

Edging - is the practice of taking your partner to the edge, but never really letting them come to orgasm, even when they are ready

Rough Sex - rough sex refers to sexual activity that involves some form of aggressive behavior, such as hair pulling, spanking, choking, slapping, hitting, and forcing someone to have sex

Anal Sex - a form of sexual activity in which the partner's penis penetrates the anus

Dirty Talk - Dirty talk is the use of graphic word images to increase sexual pleasure before and during intercourse. It is usually a part of foreplay. Dirty talk can include graphic erotic descriptions, sexual humor, sexual commands, and naughty words.

Spanking - tthe act of slapping someone with the hand, usually several times on the buttocks as punishment or for sexual gratification - e.g. - "You've been a bad girl, haven't you?' *spank*

Gagging - A sexual act in which a partner's satisfaction is enhanced by forcibly causing a partner to choke or suffocate on his erect penis

Orgasm Control - Orgasm control can mean any of several sexual activities in which orgasm is forced, denied, delayed, or prolonged, sometimes in combination with all of these ways

Ruined Orgasm - the ruined orgasm is the result of stop-and-start stimulation and teasing, without the partners control - giving the tied partner a handjob and stopping immediately when he starts to ejaculate

Tease and Denial - Tease and Denial is the sexual technique of bringing your partner close to orgasm and then stopping or reducing the stimulation to prevent orgasm from occurring.

Humiliation - In erotic humiliation, a person is humiliated during a sexual act. This type of humiliation can be either verbal, such as insulting the partner, calling them a "slut' or "bitch', or physical, such as spitting on the partner or forcing them to do something humiliating, such as kissing your feet.

Praise kink - A praise kink is when a person derives sexual pleasure from being praised. It' is sometimes known asa good girl/boy/pet kink. The person being praised is into nice words and compliments - "You're doing so well taking my cock" or "You're so beautiful when you..."

Degradation kink - Degradation Kink is the practice of using derogatory names and expressions to humiliate and degrade one's partner during sex - as "whore', "my bitch," etc. It can also include choking, holding, hitting and punishing or tying up

Definitions of Kinks and Fetishes

ONLY FOR BRAVE ONES

Tied Up - It means that either the hands or the feet or all of them are tied together or, more typically, tied to different corners or railings of the bed and you are fixed in one place for the duration of sex. Usually ropes, scarves, ribbons or even handcuffs are used.

Rim Job - An act of sexual stimulation of another person's anus with the tongue.

Hot Wax play - Have your partner drip wax from a hot candle onto your skin. This causes a slight burning sensation and can increase pleasure. We recommend using the candle on your belly, chest, or breast

Heat Play - a form of BDSM sensual play in which objects and substances are used to stimulate the body's neuroreceptors for heat for sensual effects. One can use wax, or hot tea bags, warm towels, hot sex toys, etc. for this purpose.

Cold Play - The opposite of heat play. You can tease your partner with ice cubes, chill your sex toys, or bring cold food.

Golden Shower - People who like this type of play get aroused when they piss on their partner's body as part of foreplay. Some people prefer the opposite - they love it when their partner pisses on them

Discomfort during sex - unpleasant feeling as a counterpoint to pleasure - the rough edge of a table, cold stone against the hot body; the position is unpleasant at first, but then becomes perfect.

Sweat - Try to have sex when you are both sweaty and sticky. A good time is after a workout or a hot day

Multiple Orgasms - Multiple orgasms are generally understood to be more than one orgasm in a single sex session. Try to give your partner more than one orgasm during sex. Also, try during the BDSM session and give your partner a handjob right after he comes.

Watching Porn - Select a category and a porn video you want to watch with your partner or choose it randomly. You can just watch it or replay it right after.

Rim Job - An act of sexual stimulation of another person's anus with the tongue.

FUCK ME HARD

Face Slapping - It belongs to the BDSM family and involves blows to the face of the submissive partner - e.g. as punishment

Choking - the act of strangling someone for sexual pleasure. Your partner can do this during a rough sex session by grabbing your neck for a few seconds

Fighting Sex - A sex fight is a form of sex play in which each partner tries to bring the other to orgasm first, with the partner who orgasms first being the loser. We recommend starting standing up and putting on all clothes

Scratching - Bboth of You can lightly scratch the partner's back or dig their nails into his/her shoulders and buttocks. Scratching is a way to show your partner how much passion you feel. Also, it is a small reminder that lasts for a few hours afterwards

Loud Sex - Make loud noises with your partner at the same time. Usually it is shouting "FUCK ME, DONT STOP, HARDER, HARDER", "OMG... FUCK ME. HARDER.. UH, UH, UH, COMMON, DO IT... YES... UH HUH"

DEFINITIONS OF KINKS AND FETISHES

Hate Sex - Pretend that you and your partner hate each other. Have rough sex with hair pulling, back scratching, biting, calling each other names with inappropriate words, etc.

Power Play - Power plays refer to dominant/submissive roles often acted out in the BDSM community. In these relationships, the submissive partner agrees to give up all control, to submit and obey the dominant partner. What happens after that - 'bondage, spanking, hard sex, or something even kinkier - is entirely up to you.

Breath Play - Breath-play involves the restriction of oxygen to increase erotic play or intensify an orgasm or sexual experience, and is a very risky sex act. We recommend doing it only with safe words.

CBT - CBT stands for cock and ball torture, a sexual activity in which the partner's penis or testicles are treated with pain or constriction. It may involve penis and testicle slapping, scratching, or the use of an electric wand.

Punishments - BDSM punishments can be roughly divided into painful and painless punishments. Painful punishments usually involve direct touching, such as spanking, restraint, handcuffing, etc. Non-painful punishments are often less direct, such as humiliation, which can be triggered by various verbal or physical humiliations, depending on what they personally find humiliating. We recommend punishments such as bondage, chastity, orgasm control, edging and denial or spanking.

Face-fucking - act of inserting the penis into the partner's mouth. It' is similar to oral sex, but the partner doesn't move her head in this case. She takes a relatively passive role with her mouth open and her partner moves her head back and forth

Fisting - The desire to insert a fist into the anus or vagina. Remember that without adequate lubrication, the act can be both painful and harmful.

Pegging - Pegging is a sexual practice in which the female partner performs anal sex with the male partner by penetrating his anus with a strap-on dildo

Boobs Torture - It may include breast bondage with ropes and the like, nipple clamps, slapping or whipping the breasts, hot wax, ice cubes, biting and pinching.

Forced Sex - sexual role-playing in which one partner plays the submissive (the victim) and the other the dominant (the aggressor). A r*pe fantasy in which one imagines or pretends to be forced into sexual acts.

YOU ARE UNIQUE

Sensation Play - Tthis type of play is a sensual softcore subcategory of BDSM. The partner can stimulate your sensations with silk scarves, feathers, ice or massage oils.

WAM Play - The acronym stands for "Wet and Messy" Lovers of this type of play love to apply messy substances with different textures to their own or their partner's skin. It can be whipped cream, raw eggs, milk, lotion, paint, oil, mud, pudding, chocolate sauce, fruit juice, beer, shaving cream, shampoo, soap, ketchup, ice cream, peanut butter, slime, etc. - the best place for this is a bathtub or shower.

Body painting - Geting excited about painting your partner's body or being painted. You can paint each other's bodies or just have fun with the brush and use it on your partner's nipples or pussy/dick.

Shibari - or Japanese bondage is the act of tying up a person for aesthetic purposes. Shibari is characterized by its visual aesthetics and emphasis on the emotional and psychological connection between the participants.

Nyotaimori - often referred to as "body sushi" is the Japanese practice of serving sashimi or sushi made from a woman's naked body. You can try it with your partner, even with different types of food - like whipped cream and strawberries

DEFINITIONS OF KINKS AND FETISHES

Ahegao - an exaggerated facial expression of women during sex, typically with eyes rolling or crossed, tongue out, and face slightly flushed to show pleasure or ecstasy.

Food Play - Playing with food can involve eating off your partner's body or smearing and licking the snack into your skin. You can use whipped cream or chocolate to spread on your partner and lick it off

Cyber Sex - An erotic communication between two people online via text, audio or video with the exchange of sexual messages or images with another person. You can try sex via webcams with your partner or sexting as part of foreplay.

JOI - The acronym stands for jerk-off statements. The partner becomes sexually aroused when an "instructor" gives sexual instructions. For example, what and how to masturbate, and even when to orgasm. The instructor cannot touch his/her partner, he/she can only use words.

Body Worship - is any practice of physical worship of a part of a partner's body and is usually performed as a submissive act in the context of BDSM, e.g., desire for kissing feet, penis sucking, etc.

Coming without being touched - Drive the partner crazy with words (dirty talk), gestures (e.g. sucking on your own fingers) and touching his frenulum with objects (e.g. a small brush) and stop immediately when he pretends to cum

Erotic Furniture - Also known as sex furniture, is any furniture that serves as an aid to sexual activity

MY PREFERENCES

A Top A top is someone who prefers to be in control during sex. Tops generally prefer to take a more active role in sex, acting as the person who penetrates, gives oral sex, or performs other sexual acts

A Bottom - Bottoms typically like to receive during sex, whether that means oral sex, penetration or other sexual acts.

DDLG - DDLG, or DD /LG, is an acronym for Daddy Dom/Little Girl, a sexual relationship in which the dominant man is the father figure and the woman plays the role of the young girl

MDLB - is an acronym for Mommy Dom/Little Boy. It' is when during sexual intercourse a woman acts as the dominant "mother" while the man plays the role of the submissive "little boy".

24/7 - 24/7 means 24 hours a day, 7 days a week. In BDSM, it means that the power exchange relationship is on a full-time and often live-in basis. We recommend trying this out as a SUB /DOM role with commands and sex toys for one or more days.

Dominant - Sexual dominance is a sexual practice in which one partner (called "Dom") holds power during a sexual encounter and determines the experience for the submissive partner (called "Sub"). Both partners receive sexual pleasure and satisfaction from performing their role (whether dominant or submissive) during the sexual encounter.

Submissive - Submissiveness may be limited to sex if the submissive partner experiences masochism, bondage, or other forms of dominance. However, there are also submissive people who don't limit their submission to the bedroom, but live as 'lifestyle' submissives.

Pet Play - The submissive partner goes into the fantasy of an animal to satisfy the dominant. The submissive usually plays the role of a dog, cat or cow. Collars, cages and commands are usually used.

Slave - a person who is held in a place he cannot leave and is forced to perform sexual acts.

Sugar Daddy/ Mommy - a wealthy man/woman who spends a lot of money on a younger person, in return for sexual intimacy

Switch - SWITCH means "both dominant and submissive" Switch is a term used in sexual relationships to describe a person who enjoys both the dominant (dom) and submissive (sub) roles.

DEFINITIONS OF KINKS AND FETISHES

SEX TOYS

Rabbit Vibrator - A Rabbit vibrator is a dual action sex toy that provides simultaneous penetration and clitoral stimulation

Wand Vibrator - A wand vibrator is a massage device that is often used as a vibrator and sex toy. It consists of a round vibrating bullet attached to a handle. You can use it for both pussy and penis stimulation

Vibrating Panties - Vibrating panties are simply panties that contain a bullet vibrator that connects wirelessly to a remote control. Great toy for outdoor play!

Dildo - a dildo is an object shaped like a penis that can be used to feel sexual pleasure. Can be used for both men and women

Anal Plug - A butt plug is a sex toy that is inserted into the rectum for sexual gratification. It can be used for both men and women

Penis Ring - Cock rings are rings worn around the base of the penis and sometimes around the testicles to enhance erection

SEX POSITIONS

Cowgirl - or girl-on-top means that the male partner lies on his back with his legs stretched out while the female partner straddles him.

Missionary - The missionary position or man-up position is a sex position in which generally the woman lies on her back and the man lies on top of her

69 - this position is an oral sex position where two partners give each other oral sex at the same time

Doggy Style - Doggy style is a sex position where the male partner stands or kneels behind his partner and the female partner is on all fours

Face-Off - the male Partner starts by sitting on a comfortable chair or the edge of the bed. The female Partner climbs onto their lap, straddling them, and wraps their arms around the male partner's back

Definitions of Kinks and Fetishes

BDSM SEX TOYS

Collar - A collar is a restraint that is sometimes placed around the neck of the submissive partner during BDSM play

Blindfold - Blindfolds can be used to heighten a partner's senses during sex play. They are often used in light bondage practices

Belt - This is not a typical sex toy, but we recommend using it during BDSM sessions - to tie your hands, as a spanking tool or as a collar

Handcuffs - Bondage cuffs are restraints designed for use in sexual bondage situations. Compared to traditional handcuffs, they are wide hand and ankle restraints, generally made of leather

Ropes - use a synthetic bondage rope - it has a very different interlocking than a cotton rope or a natural fibre. They are adapted to the human skin.

Tape - Bondage Tape is a 2-3 inch wide strip of thin plastic that sticks only to itself, without any adhesive, and it does not stick to the hair or skin

Zip Tie - always have a cable tie with you. This is the fastest way to catch your partner off guard, tie his hands or ankles and use it for your pleasure. Again, our great recommendation

Whip - The whip is a long, thin leather sex toy often used to inflict pain or pleasure on a partner. Pain releases endorphins in the brain, and many people use painful sex toys like whips to increase sexual pleasure.

Chastity - Chastity is fairly common in the BDSM community. For the most part, they deliver what they promise - locking your partner's penis in a cage to prevent them from masturbating, having sex, or even getting a full erection. Great toys for femdom role play

Ball Gag - A rubber ball attached to a collar that the man or woman can bite or suck on during sexual activity

Open-mouth Gag - open mouth gags are used to keep the mouth open so that the wearer can perform oral sex

Electro Play Toys - Toy that uses electricity to stimulate the nerves of the body, especially the genitals, using a power source (such as neon rods, violet rods, and TENS) for the purpose of sexual stimulation

Ass Hook - When you have an anal hook inside you, you are usually in a hogtie position with a rope connecting the anal hook to another part of your body. (This may include your hands tied behind your back, your ankles, etc.)

Printed in Great Britain
by Amazon

23292933R00020